The journey of the mage outcast

(Book 1)

By

Samson Excel

Copyright © 2022 Samson Excel

All rights reserved.

ISBN: 9798835602674

DEDICATION

I solely dedicate this book to all my friends and family that supported me during the period I engaged in this book.

CONTENTS

   Introduction   i

1 **College Drill**   Pg 1

2 **Friends and spell**   Pg 14

3 **Encounter**   Pg 25

4 **Conversation**   Pg 32

5 **The Breakout**   Pg 40

6 **Assassinations and Exposure**   Pg 49

Introduction

The flow of magic

Natural magic was exciting until nature granted some individuals the ability to harness all forms of magic. Some did well with such abilities but trust me when I say the bad ones are always more because power can be really toxic.

It takes great power to defeat great power and that's where the story Michael Leadborn comes in. Born with the special ability to harness all forms of elemental magic. His parents are forced to isolate themselves so as not to gain attention from the high council of mages, but with great power comes great responsibility and for one destined for greatness, isolation can't be a solution for ever. Attaining the age of 19 an incident occurs at the Central High mage college giving nature the opportunity to unveil itself. Surely this draw the attention of the high mages who sought to put Michael down but after much consideration they see him as a useful weapon against their believed terror Jordan Dorcana a synonymous natural executioner of all forms of natural elemental magic but evil by nature. Jamir one of the high council's most powerful mage guardians is given the privilege to train Michael ahead of what is to come.

As we proceed in this journey of great fantasy, action and thriller we get to encounter many more experience witnessed by Michael, even his amazing encounter with Celine Mcgrof who later becomes his source of motivation and strength ahead of what is too come.

BOOK TITLE

College Drill

(***"Bell rings, lot of chattering can be heard, the noises of both fresh men and senior mages can be identified through the atmosphere. It's the beginning of the summer session and a lot are to be expected......mind you am the narrator not the protagonist and I will be guiding us through this fantastic journey***"(*"giggles for a while"*).

Just after being granted admission into the Central High Mage College, Michael stands as he gazes at the enormous structures in his presence. He still can't believe that he is far away from home, Stuck with his experience of living in isolation with few friends and little communication with the outside world He still seems surprised at himself and his parents for letting him accept the decision of moving out from home and going to college not just any college but Central High Mage college.

But he plans to keep all that behind, start a fresh life and make the best out of his stay at Central High but isn't that what we all say as freshmen("chuckles") but he couldn't be blamed weighing on the fact on what he has been through.

As he makes his way towards the registration room, he is greeted by so many faces which make him surprised but happy at the same time. Getting close to his destination he bumps into a red haired fellow by name Marcus Ruff,
"*I am sorry I didn't see you coming*" Michael said as he helped him pick up his books from the floor,
 "*It's all good guess I was lost in my thoughts, am Marcus, Marcus Ruff and you are?*" he replied.
 "*You mean like the Ruff family, like the popular Ruff family?* Michael replied astonished.
"yea *the popular one*" he replied sluggishly
"*what's so intriguing about my family name, all*

those stuffs about them are history can't we just be treated with the present" he said with a pale look on his face.

"You guys are legends, cmon one can't easily neglect history especially when it involves saving the world" Michael said smiling.

"Whatever I just don't like being evaluated with my family's name" he replied grumpily.

"Ok fine I get it, am Michael by the way nice to meet you" Michael replied.

"So where are you from Michael?, you don't seem to be from around here, can tell from the way you react to some stuffs" Marcus asked.

"Naah, South West Yorkshire, little riverside area close to the mountains really far from the city" Michael replied slowly. *"wow, you are really far from home man"* Marcus laughed, *"but welcome to Bringsburgh man, guess I'll give you a tour around the school"* he added.

"lol, I'll really appreciate that Michael said(*"oh my gosh, am getting my college tour by Marcus Ruff, like an actual Ruff"* Michael said in his mind loudly).

"Have you been assigned a house yet?" Marcus asked. *"Naah, the queue is kinda long; I think I'll wait"* Michael replied. *"Are you a senior?"* Michael added.

"*lol, 2^(nd) year, let's sought out your assigning issues come with me*" Marcus said.
And so he followed Marcus towards the assigning room, "*hey Brad, my pal here needs a house could you assign one to him* "Marcus said and winked at Michael",
"*Sure Marcus what's his name?*" Brad asked.
"*Michael, Michael Lead born*" Michael replied.
"*Ok, Michael step into the circle*" Brad said.
"*What circle?*" Michael asked trying to navigate the room.

(Now it was a tradition for the circle of brimstone to assign a house to new intakes in the college according to their strength, skill and character. The four houses of Central High Mage College included (Phoenix, Dragon, Griffin and Serpent each with their characteristics).

"*The circle towards the north door*" Brad answered.
Looking towards the north door his eyes came across a carved circle on the floor,
"*This one*" Michael asked pointing towards it.
"*Yea that one, just stand at the middle*" Brad replied.

And so he moved towards the circle and stood at the middle "what *next*" he asked looking towards their direction.

"Say *this words* "thy **belief in thy making till I am certain that I made it**" Brad spoke.

"Thy belief in thy making till I am certain that I made it" Michael spoke firmly.

(**Suddenly there was an outburst of light which was so bright that no one could see a thing, and at that moment it was quite obvious as to which house he has been given, and off course we were right Phoenix it was certainly cause such emission of power only occurred during such circumstances.)**

"Why are you guys looking at me like that" Michael asked surprised.

"Phoenix is rare, only those who harness great power are given the opportunity to be amongst them. Guess your one lucky powerful fellow my friend "Marcus told him with a powerful smile on his face as he lead him away from the starring audience but Michael kept on saying within himself " *I hope they*

don't know about what I am or else am done for".

"Aiit, we'll be meeting with your house leader so you can know your room, I'll see you during lunch at the banquet hall" Marcus said as he looked towards his right.

"Hey, hello are you here? Did you hear any word I just spoke man" Marcus added waving at Michael's face, guess Marcus noticed Michael was lost at the moment. What's bothering you" Marcus asked.

"ohh sorry, my bad, nothing am fine you said we're meeting with my house leader right, ok nice where do we do that?"Michael asked.

"Man it's not even up to a day and your already down, cheer up your gonna love this place with time". Marcus laughed. "lol, ok I feel you". Michael replied.

And so they both walked down the hall way towards the dorm arena,

*"Hey Jordi, have you seen Thomas?" Marcus asked a female student sitting close to the quadrangle close to the dorm, her eyes were green and she was really pretty, like wow (**aiit, I should get back to the story**").*

"He's *upstairs, his room which you know, what's up, are you in trouble now?*" She asked with a stern look.

"*cmon, must I be in trouble before I get to look for Thomas*" Marcus laughed.

"*Who is the new kid, and why are you trying to influence him*", she turned to Michael "*stay away from him, he is trouble*" she said.

"*lol, I can handle trouble if you're worried about that*" Michael replied smiling.

"*Tough guy right, guess Marcus recruitment process keeps getting better, don't say I didn't warn you*" she said.

"*hey, cmon don't give the lad a bad impression about me, be nice love*" Marcus laughed.

"*Whatever*" she said.

So we made our way towards the dorm staircase, Thomas resided on the 4th floor which was way up, "*so you're trouble*" Michael asked smiling.

"*Lol, sometimes, if you live 100 percent by the rules trust me you would easily die of boredom*" Marcus answered smiling.

"*Interesting*" Michael thought within himself smiling mischievously.

" *naah, I know that smile don't even think about doing something crazy, I get away cause of my family name, you might not*" Marcus said.

"*cmon, it was nothing*" Michael laughed.

 "*it better be*" Marcus replied unconvinced.

"*Room 292, I believe that's supposed to be his room*" Marcus said like he was unsure of what he was doing.

"*You don't know his room* "Michael asked seemingly a little bit surprised, "*you would have asked her?*"He added.

"Don't *worry I know what am doing*" Marcus said forcing a fake smile on his face.

And so we walked and walked through the dorm floors, it looked as if we were trying to get a picture of the whole dorm. *"Yes! Found it, I knew I could do this*" Marcus laughed.

 ""*thank Mother Nature cause I was almost about to give up*" Michael replied with a relieved tone.

("**Knock knock"), ("knock, knock"), ("knock, knock").**

"*I think that's enough, he must have heard that I believe*" Michael said looking at Marcus like he was a nuisance. "*c'mon, the best way to get him out is by annoyance, touching the tiger's tail you know"* he said smiling mischievously.

"Who is that!!!!" answered from behind the door.

"OK, that was fierce, guess you just succeeded in pissing him off" Michael said.

("**Door opens**")

"Marcus, I am gonna kill you one day just believe, what do you want?" Thomas said, (**really tall brown-haired looking fellow, he wasn't bad for a house leader if I was to judge with his appearance**).

"cmon man, that's no way to greet a friend" Marcus laughed.

"lol, what's up man, what trouble have you gotten yourself into now" Thomas said laughing as they embraced themselves, Michael must have been surprised from Thomas reaction at moment cause of his attitude at first.

"New kid man, he's a phoenix surprisingly" Marcus said smiling.

" really, it's been long we had a new member, guess Fortune decided to favour us "Thomas said surprised, *" what's your name fellow?"* Thomas asked.

"Michael, Michael Leadborn" Michael replied. *"alright Michael let's get you a place, I believe you must know my name but I'll be introducing myself, I am Thomas Burton and I am your house leader, whatever problem you encounter in college you must address to me before anyone, whatever information you require you can get from me, you'll be enlightened more on the rules and regulations guiding this sacred and prestigious house and the penalties that come with breaking such rules during the initiation ceremony tonight, that will be enough introduction from me Michael, any questions?"* Thomas asked.

"Ummmmm, none for now but maybe later". Michael replied.

"Ok, come with me, Marcus you know the drill". Thomas said looking at Marcus.

"don't *worry I'll wait here*" Marcus said. "*Why can't he come with us?*" Michael asked.

"Griffin's or any other house can't step into Phoenix territory same way we can't to theirs, territorial rule, always remember that, the only reason he got this was because of my

supremacy in this house" Thomas said with a stern look.

"Ok here we are, room 224, here is your key, you can get unpacked now and feel relaxed we are one family here, I'll see you at the initiation ground tonight". Thomas spoke.
"Thank you, am really grateful" Michael replied.

With that he left, unlocking the room, its appearance wasn't that bad, seemed like it was newly vacated, but that's not my worry, I just get unpacked and rest before the ceremony Michael thought within himself.
 "Hello, am Philip your neighbour, nice to meet you" came a voice from the door.
 "I am Michael" Michael said looking towards the door as he was met with the appearance of a young fellow who seemed like his age grade.
⁶*"do you need help unpacking"* Philip asked.
 "No *I'm good thanks* "Michael replied.
"Alright if you need anything am next door" Philip said smiling as he walked out.
 "Are you going for the ceremony?" Michael asked.

"Yea, *are you not coming?*" he replied
"*I am, just wanted to ask you to inform me when you're going so I could come along, don't really know the venue*" Michael said.
"*Ok I'll certainly do that man*" Philip said as he moved out.
And so Michael decided to rest off as he waited for nightfall to come. He fell asleep only to be woken by a knock his door,
"*Who is there*" Michael asked.
"hey *we are going to be late, I have been knocking since*" came Philip's voice from across the door.
"*Oh my am sorry, I slept off, give me a second*" Michael said as he sprang out from his bed. (Stepping out from his room) "Am *really sorry for the delay*" Michael apologised.
"*It's ok let's get moving or we'll be late*" Philip replied.

(**Music could be heard from afar, a lot of shouting and laughing, huge bonfires and various scary decorations, it was a scene but a wonderful one to behold. Suddenly music stopped and everywhere went still then a loud noise came from the podium).**

"Griffins, Serpents, Dragons and Phoenixes welcome". Now that was the clan leader talking (clan leaders perform the duties of student president, he overran the activities of the students in a particular college).

"freshmen step forward, welcome to Central High Mage College, from now henceforth you are all special mages and you should treat yourself as such, you would be handed a manual containing the rules and regulations that will be guiding your stay in this college. Penalties are also included and trust me when I say they will be executed accordingly just as you will see in your various manuals, without further much ado, we the senior mages at Central High Mage College welcome you all into our clan and we accept you all as one of us..........now who is ready to party!!!!". He shouted with much excitement.

You could hear screams from far and wide. It was such a blissful night, what a way to end your first day in college.

Friends and spell

It has been three months since resumption, lot of activities to be involved in, and classes to partake in and spell training to undergo. But I guess all these are prices student gats to pay to be one of the best at Central High Mage College.

A few friends had been added to Michael's friends list, exposure to various activities allowed him to interact with new set of people and attain new forms of ideas. He seemed to be adjusting pretty well both socially and educationally but trust me when I say behind every smooth sail there must be a storm and in this situation Devon Lark was his storm.

Born in a prestigious family, he always had what he wanted which made him addicted to getting people fulfil his wishes by whatever means necessary. Now he felt like he was experiencing a rebellion because Michael never agreed to any of his ideas and practices, this he saw as a challenge and as so swore to make life miserable for him.

(*"Now I guess Michael's three months of happiness was about to come to an end"*).

(*"A lot of noises could be heard, either those making a jest of others, or those associated with the discussion unit or probably the first year spell unit, you could still feel your environment enclosed with vocal sounds"*).

"Hey *Michael hurry up, you guys too or we would be in Professor Kathryn's red book*" Claire shouted as she ran towards the spell theatre.
"*Were coming*" shouted Lizzy, Gerald and Michael as they ran to meet up with him.

(*Lizzy Brown(Griffin student), Gerald Bane(,Dragon student) and Claire Kingston(Serpent student) all freshmen were the new friends Michael had added to his friends list and they seemed to be getting along pretty fine*).

"Ok, listen up young mages" echoed professor Kathryn's voice from the back door, *"we're going to be practicing controls. Select a partner and place a cup of water on his or her head, I need any of you to lift the cup of water from his or her head and place it on the floor without spilling it, and if you're successful your wristbands go green and you're good to go. Now let's get started".* She commanded.

"Lizzy let's do this" Michael said smiling at Gerald.
"Cmon, I can't be stuck with Claire " Gerald cried out in dismay.
"What's that supposed to mean Gerald, are you calling me a good for nothing, did you picture me as a weakling" Claire answered with some sought of anger in her voice.
"Cmon, I was kidding, I wouldn't dare do that my princess" Gerald said forcing a smile on his face.
"You better be" Claire replied.

Michael and Lizzy couldn't help laughing about the situation on ground.

"It's *not funny*" Gerald said sternly.

"*We're sorry*" Michael replied, "have fun out there" Michael said jokingly.

"*Alright, who is going first you or i?*" Michael asked Lizzy.
"*emm, I think I'll start this one*" Lizzy replied smiling.
"you *have three attempts, then I'll go*" Michael said as he filled up his cup with water and placed it on his head.

(Splash, Splash, Splash went the water from Michael's cup on him thrice, and this point he was all soaked up)

"*Am sorry*" replied Lizzy trying so hard to withhold her laughter, "*I just can't get it up with ease. It feels kinda heavy whenever I try*". She added
"so *spilling it on me is the best option, nice*" Michael replied smiling.
"I *know your gonna do the same, am sorry*" she cried laughing.
"Naah, *don't worries I don't pay evil for evil, am a good guy remember*" Michael replied smiling mischievously.
"I *don't believe you*" Lizzy said still laughing.

"Am *serious, trust me*" Michael answered.

(Splash came the water from Lizzy cup on his first attempt)
"*I hate you*" Lizzy said laughing.
"Cmon, *relax two more still to come*" Michael said looking away.

(Splash came the 2nd cup of water on Lizzy)
"*HahahaHahaha, look at your face*" Michael said laughing.
"*Am going to kill u after this*" she replied with her face twitched up.
"*Alright I'll try not to spill it this time* "Michael said smiling
(And slowly as he focused his attention on the cup, he could feel the elemental force of water running through his veins and with which he direct towards the cup and was able to place it on the floor and at an instance their wristbands went green indicating qualification).

"*Lol, how did you do that*" Lizzy asked.

"I *guess I just needed to focus more, I could feel the energy running through me"* Michael said as he surveyed the surface of his arms.

"hmmm, *so am guessing you are a water elemental mage"* she said.
"I *don't really think so, water isn't really my thing* "Michael replied.
"it *could be, you just probably might not have figured it out"* Lizzy said.

"Have *you figured out yours?"* Michael asked.
" *I have this strong connection with air, lol there was a period a guy tried to bully me back in high school I was so terrified and angry at the same time, I flung him out of my class with huge amount of air. I think I broke his leg, I felt so relieved after that. Don't call me evil cause is not I just reacted to my environment.* Lizzy answered smiling.
"Lol *that's dope, I wouldn't mind attempting that on Devon Lark*" Michael said "*such an annoying fellow"* Michael added.

(And when you speak about the devil, trust me you always draw his attention)

"Hey Michael, how did you cheat your way through this test or lemme guess your blond maidservant did the work for you?!!" Devon shouted from across the theatre hall.

(There **was a total outburst of laughter inside the hall; guess Professor Kathryn was available to witness this**).

"What did he just call me; did he just call me a maidservant?" Lizzy said angrily as she attempted to go and confront Devon but Michael held her back saying " hey cmon, don't let him get into your head, by the way he is a water elemental mage so this is his turf, you're no match for him just ignore".

" hey Blondie, did he just tell you what to do and you just did, lol guess you were more of a slave than I thought" Devon said " or are you his personal Slut" he added slowly.

(**Uhhhhhhhhhhhh came echoes from the theatre hall, that was really intense**)

" That's it, I've had enough" Lizzy said as she stood up angrily " hey Devon, you big headed *water freak, do you at times get to check mate yourself before you try to intimidate other fellas whom you are aware are 100 times better than you are, guess it must be difficult for you to adapt here especially when you lack attention for your freak nature and at such you try to create one for yourself but trust me freak, nobody loves a freak, stupid!!!"* Lizzy shouted.

(Ok, **I didn't expect that, silence swept through the entire theatre floor as no expected such reaction from. Now the next thing on our minds was what Devon is going to do now)**

"*lol, what did you just call me Blondie"* Devon asked with a sharp tone.
"You *heard me, FREAK*" Lizzy answered in the same manner.

And all of a sudden icy spikes were sent flying towards Lizzy direction.
(**My goodness was he trying to kill her; this dude must be really crazy).**

Lizzy stood in shock as she caught a glimpse of her life fading before her. **Splash**!!! Came water pouring upon her and she thought to herself what just happened?

"I wouldn't attempt that again "Michael said as he melted the remaining forms of icy spikes. "Seems *like we've got ourselves a challenge"* Devon said smiling mischievously.

(At that it was obvious what was about to happen, of course you guessed right Mage Brawl.)

"Michael, you don't have to this" Lizzy said in a sad tone.
"If you had listened, probably I wouldn't "Michael replied "go *upstairs I'll be fine"* he added.

Everyone had scampered to the upper side of the theatre, now the lower floor was open to battle.
Down came icy spikes rainy on Michael instantly and continuously but Michael was quick in response as to adjust to a defensive position and continuously melted all spikes

that were thrown at him. This continued for more than an hour and everyone was of the conclusion that Michael was so going to wear out and give in to Devon's attack but unknown to them it was all but an endurance strategy used to wear Devon out.

"Hey *cowards are you going to go defensive in this, that's no fun man*" Devon said mockingly.

"*not really I was just waiting for the perfect time to launch an attack*" said Michael as he commanded a wave of water of which it's sight was unbelievable to both Devon and everyone at the upper floor and down came the wave upon Devon almost drowning him and at that moment, Prof Kathryn stepped in.

"My *goodness what just happened here, is that Devon laying on the floor, Michael what you have done*" Prof Kathryn cried.

"He *attacked me Ma, I only responded in self defence*" Michael replied.

"By *trying to drown him, detention right away, the rest of you are dismissed*" Prof Kathryn shouted.

"*But Ma he wasn't at fault*" Lizzy, Gerald and Claire shouted in Michael's defence.

"*I said you all are dismissed*" Prof Kathryn said looking sternly at them.

"Hey *guys its ok, I'll be fine. Guess he won't be bothering any of us again"* Michael said smiling as he walked towards the detention Hall.

Encounter

(It was week two of Michael's three weeks detention and trust me it wasn't funny at all, routine sanitation activities and solo library reading wasn't something you would want to try, you could die of either stress or boredom trust me. But sometimes not all bad things are bad you know. For Michael, it was within this situation that he met her, his adventurous and ambitious female mage with no other identity than that of Celine Mcgrof, daughter of High chief mage Zerock Mcgrof leader of the High Mage Council)....

Stepping into the library hall for his normal solo reading which was a condition in his detention Michael is surprised to see a living human figure at his normal reading spot in the library.

"*Ok that's weird, I don't normally get visitors during solo reading periods*" Michael said to himself as he approached the entity in his midst

"Ok she's female, I guess another detention recruit" he added.

"*Ehemmmm(coughing), excuse me Ma'am you're sitting on my spot*" Michael said.
She looked up and smiled and then asked "*what's your name please?*".
"*Michael, any problem?* Michael said with curiosity.
She looked to her left and then slowly to her right and repeated the same action like she was in search of something.
"*Are you looking for anything*" Michael asked with the intent of helping.
"*Oh yea, your name on the seat but I guess I can't find it cause your name isn't on it*" she said smiling mischievously.
At that moment Michael was dumbfounded, he was feeling kinda stupid at that moment.
"*I know your butt ain't bigger than the benches so we could easily share no hard feelings I just love the spot*" Celine said
"*Am Celine*" she added as Michael sat close to her.

"Nice to meet you" Michael said forcing a smile on his face and he was still trying to get over the humiliation he just experienced now. *"Am sorry for how our introduction went but never ask a lady to stand for a guy, cmon you should be a gentleman"* Celine said.
"Fair" Michael replied.
"So how long have you been here?" Celine asked.
"This is my second week" Michael replied *"what are you doing here?"* he added.
"Got busted so I was sent here " she answered.
"lol, busted like you attempted robbery or what?" Michael asked with curiosity.
"Robbery, cmon!!" she laughed *" it was more like from a failed breakout to Serac"* she added.
"Wait what!!! Serac are you crazy, why would you want to go to somewhere that dangerous!!"
Michael exclaimed.
"Hey, no need for drama, why are all scared of Serac, have you ever been there or have you ever seen someone who complained of that place being haunted or cursed

?, all those stories are just to keep us out cause they have something hidden down there that they don't want we college mages to be aware of" Celine said sharply.

"OK *maybe, just maybe you might have a point but that doesn't mean we should still ignore instructions given to us"* Michael said.

"OK *good one, you can decide to live in a lie but as for me I am addicted to the truth"* Celine said.

"*You couldn't have pulled out a breakout alone, so where are your accomplices?*" Michael asked.

"*I took the fall for all of them, it was my idea so I had too even though the failure of the plan wasn't"* she replied.

"Lol, *the failure wasn't, care to explain cause I think am beginning to enjoy this, you mean to say you might have had a successful breakout if someone hadn't messed up?*" Michael asked.

"*lol you are smart, according to my calculations, certainly"* she answered.

"So *what happened?"* Michael replied with another question.

"Hope *you're not a snitch?"* she said looking at me in a curious manner.

"lol, *am not*" Michael replied smiling.

"*ok, I feel like I can trust you cause if this gets out my friends would be in serious trouble and I'll come for your head, trust me*" she said in a rough threatening manner.

"Lol, *ok boss I won't trust me*" he said laughing at her reaction.

"OK, *we're good*" she said smiling. "*well we're supposed to breakout from the northern sector, we had both our timing and required spells in check both our positioning was the problem we encountered, a friend of my was supposed to position himself at Grey North quarters for our teleportation spell to work but mistook it for May Front quarters which go our spell wrong and there were enhancements made to the security system which enabled it to detect our spell whereas triggering the security alarm. Not all of us could get away safely so I had to create a diversion to enable my friends escape and Woow!!! Here I am*" she explained. "What *about you?*" she added.

"Well *I got into a fight with Devon Lark*" Michael answered.

"*Lol, like Devon Lark the bully, are you crazy? Guess he beat the shit out of you and you found yourself in detention*" she said laughing.

"*I actually almost killed him, nearly drowned him to death*" Michael replied smiling.

"*you're joking, not the Devon I know*" she said looking at me "*you're serious*" she added now looking at me intently, "*how did you pull that off, cmon!!*" she exclaimed.

"*well I just faced like he was a normal dude and ended up almost killing him, something I intend on not trying again*" Michael answered.

"When *was this?*" she asked.

"Last *two weeks, during spelling test I guess you were in batch B*" Michael said

"*wait a minute, you're the popular guy who got into a fight with Devon, my gosh I couldn't believe it when I heard it, I thought my friends were joking!!!*" she said with great deal of surprise, "*am impressed, so are you a water mage or sought?* She asked.

"not really, can't really say what my deal is yet" Michael answered.

"Am *a fire mage by the way, a Dragon student as you know in case you decide to look for me after detention*" she said starring deeply into his eyes.

"lol, *I'll surely do that you know*" Michael replied.

**And so it went for days, the strong connection that was building between Michael and Celine continued growing even after she completed her detention he still thought about her. I guess he was beginning to develop feelings for her.
And so it went until his detention was completed, he could now go back to being** Micheal Leadborn".

"Freedom *is that you!!!!*" Michael exclaimed as he stepped out of the detention office.

Conversation

It has been days since Michael completed his detention process, he was back to his normal college mage routine, and of course he had a lot of catching up to do in relations to his mage courses which seemed to look like a lot of pressure and stress but for some who just completed detention stress and pressure should be nothing right? ("*Chuckles*").

"Hey *Michael, hurry up am hungry!!!*" Lizzy shouted.
"*Am sorry boss*" Michael said smiling.
"*You, you guys should wait up!!*" shouted Gerald from behind.
"*Where is Claire?*" Michael asked.
"*She left early*" Gerald answered "but *she is supposed to reserve a table for us thou*" he added.
"Ok, *she should be doing that regularly* "Michael said smiling.

"Hey *guys!*!" Claire shouted as she waved towards their direction as they entered the canteen Hall.

"*There she is* "Gerald said.

"Lizzy, *you can go on while I and Gerald get us something to eat* "Michael said.

"*Alright boys, you know my usual, don't waste my time cause I could erupt at any moment*" Lizzy said smiling.

"Yes *ma'am"* Michael said.

And so Michael and Gerald moved towards the counter so as to select what they were going to eat and suddenly Gerald starting kicking his shoe whispering

"*Hey I think Celine Mcgrof is approaching us*"

"Lol, *who is that*" Michael said with surprise in his face.

"don't *joke with me man, the hottest female freshman, bro she is really approaching us, I can't look*" Gerald said as he turned and faced the counter.

Michael turned to see who was making Gerald nervous and lo and behold it was her.

"Hey, when did you get out?" Celine said as she kissed him on the cheek.

"What *the fuck just happened now*" thought Gerald as he starred in bewilderment.

"lol, that's new" Michael said smiling

"well, *let's just say I missed you so I felt like*" Celine replied "you *didn't bother to find me?"* she added.

"I have not been out for long, was planning on doing that thou" Michael replied.

" *lemme pretend to believe that"* Celine said in a doubtful manner " *these are my friends Eugene and August* "she added.

"No *females' friends"* Michael said as he stretched forth his hands to greet them *"nice to meet you guys"*.

"*Biggest fan*" said Eugene smiling.

"This *pal Gerald, my female friends are sitting over there Lizzy and Claire"* Michael said pointing to the direction where Lizzy and Claire sat "you *wanna join us?"* he asked.

"Naah *am heading out, maybe some other time"* Celine said.

"*Alright*" Michael replied.

And so they left and Gerald was like

"Man, *you didn't tell me you had something going on with Celine, bro you are a star now"* Gerald said in a mischievous tone.

"lol, *it's nothing, I was just fortunate to observe detention with her that's all*" Michael answered.

"Man *that's crap, did you see the way she was looking at you, damn boy what spell did you use this time*" Gerald said with curiosity.

"*Bro you're crazy*" Michael said laughing "*let's get this stuff to the table, Lizzy is already gonna kill us*" he added.

Approaching their table Lizzy reacted

"So *you guys took my meal time to get a conversation with Celine Mcgrof*" Lizzy said angrily.

"Hey, *cmon we were approached by her*" Michael said in their defense.

"Whatever, *what did she want?*" Lizzy asked with curiosity

"she *is my friend, just a little catch up*" Michael replied.

"*Your friend, since when*" Lizzy asked looking surprised.

"*we served detention together and within that period we became friends*" Michael replied.

"*Friends, you're sure it's just Friends, cause she just pecked you a while ago and the way she starred at wasn't the JUST FRIENDS LOOK*" Gerald said mockingly.

"*She pecked him, wow* "Claire said starring at Michael with curiosity.

"Lol, *what's with you guys, seriously it is nothing I swear*" Michael replied laughing.

"*alright, I'll pretend to believe you for now*" Lizzy said.

And so college life went on as normal, classes and all. Reuniting with his friends was really nice but Michael was still really bother by what Celine had told him about Serac and his curiosity was becoming a burden to him, he didn't know if he could confine in his friends but in all he was willing to try.

"*hey guys, there is something I'll like to share with you guys but it has to be a secret, can I trust you guys with it*" Michael told his friends one afternoon after normal spell lectures.

"You're *dating her now, I knew it cause the way you guys have interacting lately, I just knew cmon spill it*" Lizzy replied sharply.

"*what cmon, not that it's something else*"

Michael replied laughing *"you guys should meet me at the library by 5pm"* he added.

"hmmmm ok" they all said.

And so the day went until it was 5pm and everyone turned up at the library except for Michael.

"Where is he now, I hope this isn't a prank cause I called my psyche meditation training for this" Lizzy said in a worrisome manner.

"Hey *guys, sorry am late"* echoed Michael's voice from a corner "let's *go inside"* he added.

"Alright so what's this all important meeting all about Claire asked?

"Yes, *what's up man"* Gerald added.

"Ok *this might sound crazy but it has really been bothering me. Have you guys ever wondered why we are restrained from going to Serac?"* Michael asked.

"em cmon we are told the place is haunted and who would want to go to a place that is haunted" Gerald asked.

"But we have really seen anyone who could testify to that, those were just words from the school council" Lizzy said sharply.

"*Exactly my point, I love the way you think love*" Michael said.

"*OK, even at that what are your intentions Michael*" Claire said looking at Michael with intense curiosity.

"*Well*" Michael said

"*I think Michael wants us to break out of college and go to Serac*" Lizzy said smiling "*am all in, I love this*" she added.

"* wait, what guys cmon are you guys insane, how do you guys even intend on breaking out when everywhere is tightly secured*" Gerald said in disbelief.

"*I know someone who can, Celine. She has attempted this before and based on her calculations she was right and If we add more power without strength I believe we all can do it*" Michael replied.

"*Ok I still think it is a bad idea man, I can't Claire talk sense into this dude*" Gerald said still I'm disbelief.

"Well *in as much as the idea is crazy, I wouldn't mind trying crazy*" Claire said smiling.

"*My goodness, seriously am out, don't say I

didn't warn you guys" Gerald said walking out.

"*So when do we set off?*" Lizzy asked.

"*I'll speak with Celine then I'll communicate back to you guys, please you can tell no one about this*" Michael insisted.

"*Sure alright boss*" Lizzy said smiling.

The Breakout

So after they conversation with the group at the library, Michael communicated with Celine and their intentions and trust her for a lady with an adventurous profile, she was surely going to accept. A day was arranged when both parties where going to meet up so as to be notified about the plan and after all the meetings, a plan was successful devised. Gerald on the other hand had experienced a change of heart so his was actually part of the process now. Friday May 19th was chosen as the day for the execution of the breakout because the moon would be stronger and spells were likely to be more powerful during such period. Weeks and Days had passed and finally it was already here, the night they were either gonna makes history or experience serious consequences for their actions.

"Hey you guys, by 9:30 you all should be at your positions" Celine said with much seriousness on her face *"this wristbands am gonna give you guys indicates that our positioning is all good once it goes red and that's our signal to create our portal, please if you still have doubts you could still back out now"* she added looking all around.

"OK I guess we're all in, see you all tonight" Celine said as she stood up from the canteen table where they had decided to meet that afternoon.

"This shit gonna be crazy" Gerald said as they walked back to their dorms.

"I think am in love with crazy" Claire replied as everyone busted out in laughter.

And so it was arranged, 9:30 was the time. Seems like the moon was really in their favor at that point. Everyone assembled at his or her position and when their wristband gave its notification and portal spell was casted by each one of them with a specific location in mind, boom was a flash and out they came on a lonely environmental with had beautiful trees all around it.

"ohhk are you sure we're at the right place

cause according what I have heard, Serac is meant to be all lonely, scary and haunted in nature" Lizzy said in a surprising tone

"Unless it was all but a lie" Celine replied smiling *"cmon let's explore"* she added as she slide down through the rocky paths down to the plain fields.

For Michael it was all but different, he was feeling kinda fuzzy deep within his head, it was like he felt some sort of energy emerging from the environment. Suddenly he started hearing voices inside his calling onto him; it was like he was being drawn towards the direction of those voices. Funny enough the gangs were too excited about exploration that they didn't notice Michael was missing not until Gerald tried to question him about some plants he was seeing.

"Emm guys, where Michael is" Gerald asked.

"He was just right behind us" Lizzy said in a surprised tone.

"ohhhhhk probably, just probably this place is really haunted" August said in a distressed tone.

"Shut up, probably he diverted to somewhere else, let's just look for him" Celine replied to

August in a sharp tone.

"Has anyone got anything related to Michael so I could cast a tracking spell" she asked.

"Um yea, his scarf" Lizzy said as she removed the scarf on her neck that belonged to Michael.

And so Celine casted a spell of which they followed into a strange area that had a cave like entrance with a weird inscription on the top.

"Emm I don't think we should go in, we could just shout his name from here and he will come out" August said as he stood apart in fear.

"Why you such a baby" Lizzy asked in anger *"what if he is being held by something, you would want us to alert whatever is doing that"*

"am glad someone sees you as I do" Celine said.

"I guess we are all going in" she added as she stepped into the cave like structure.

And so did everyone else cause no one wanted to be left behind and the moved they kept on hearing various sounds of different creatures. It seemed this particular strange environment was more like a prison house than a haunted ground. And so they moved till they came across a void like chamber that seemed to be a portal and suddenly the track spell stopped.

"ohhhk now this is really serious, why would Michael move as far as here and we probably don't know what lies ahead and the spell just stopped" Claire said in a distressed tone.

"Even at that we can't still leave him here, he might be in trouble and we've got to help, he would do the same if he was in our shoes" Celine said

"How can you tell, don't let your feelings for a random guy make you do something stupid" August said sharply.

"He's right Celine, cmon we barely even know this guy and we are trying to risk our lives for him "Eugene replied in support of August statement.

"Well you could leave if you want to am going in" Celine said in anger.

"ohh we're coming with you, you guys could stay and watch over the door" Gerald said as he stepped in with Celine and so did Claire

and Lizzy.

And out they came in a well defined room thst was well lighted with grey crystals and in their front was Michael talking to a grey headed guy and it looked like he was chained with black crystals!!!, like that can only be used on someone too powerful they said themselves but unknown to them the figure that was at their presence was one of the greatest threat to the mage society Lord Jordan Dorcana.

"I see you brought your friends along, come out you four let's see your faces" Dorcana said.

How did he notice our presence the said to them as they stepped out?

"What are you guys doing here" Michael said in an angry tone.

"We came to get you, you just left without informing anyone so we were worried and decided to find you. Why are you acting all hostile towards us?" replied Lizzy in a surprised tone.

"Well as you can see I don't need saving so you all can leave!!" Michael shouted.

*"no no, you all can stay. As a matter of fact he

is acting this because he doesn't want you guys to know his true identity and forgive my manners young ones my name is Lord Jordan Dorcana of whom am sure you guys must have heard or read about but do not believe those lies, I am no evil but a savior. I have been imprisoned her for 15yrs because of my vision for the future mage society and my friend you see here is no different from me. Dorcana spoke

"*I am nothing like you*" Michael shouted "don't believe a word he says he is a liar" he cried.

"*if you all have been quite observant, you must have noticed that this young fella has the ability to harness all four elemental powers of which is a sacrilege to the mage society but because he has been living a life of deceit and lies he easily fooled you all into accepting him as an ordinary mage*" Dorcana continued.

"*Is this true?*" Celine asked with tears in her eyes.

"*I couldn't tell you guys I was an outcast; I was scared any of you might betray me and sell me out*" Michael said in a sad tone." *I have lived in hiding all my life and I wasn't ready to mess up this opportunity of living a normal life*", he added.

"But we are your friends, we wouldn't sell you out for any reason, you should try to trust us a little if you believe we are really friends, I tell you everything single that's happens to me because I trust you and I expect the same, we all expect the same" Lizzy said in disappointment.

"Am sorry, I just didn't want to mess up my opportunity of having a normal life" Michael said in a sad tearful tone.

"you see young fella, people like us can't have a normal life cause we're are special, set me free and I'll help you bring out the best in you" Dorcana proposed.

"I would never, like I said I am nothing like you no matter what happens to me" Michael said.

"emm guys I think we need to leave ASAP, it does soon gonna be dawn" Gerald said in a worrisome tone.

"Alright but no one spills an atom of what happened here to anyone not even August or Eugene or any other person" Celine said with a stern voice.

And so they ran out towards the void like door and out they came and August and Eugene breathed out in relief.

"What happened" August asked looking curious.

"Nothing much, I think he was lost in his head or something" Celine replied *"we need to get out of here quickly before its dawn"* she added.

And so they ran out towards the point they had appeared and with a spell being casted with joint effort, out they were the college premises.

Assassinations and Exposure

It has been days since the gangs crazy encounter with Dorcana. Everyone was still trying to get over it and adjust to the truth that was been known, questions surrounding loyalty, lies and trust were been thrown to the sky but in all the gang had made up their mind to get through all together irrespective of whatever that might had happened.
It was the week of Azure's festival, one of their predecessors known to have helped is the dispersion of mage knowledge and culture. At least something to help put their minds at ease because a lot of preparations were involved with arrangements. But unknown to the jubilant mages it was also the appointed time Dorcana's mage cult had chosen to strike and free their saviour, a plan even Dorcana himself wasn't aware of(I guess he really made a mark before he was apprehended).

Wendy Jurant, former commander to the mage special force was actually their leader. After being dismissed unjustly for a crime that was committed by a fellow commander under the special force, she sought for a new faith and found hope in the ways of Dorcana. Her hatred for the mage council made her even stronger as she swore to leave a mark that they would never forget. 5yrs was what it took her to devise such a solid plan, with Intel from both outside and inside the college she was able to accumulate the necessary details required for the execution of this masterpiece and Azure's festival was the perfect time for this.

As time went, the day for Azure's festival came upon and of course it was a night festival. The day was used to execute massive decorations, cooking and lot's more but the night was for jubilation and feasting and that was when Wendy had decided to strike. Amidst her plans to save Dorcana, she also had intentions to execute a mass murder of which she intended to use in making her mark towards the council.

With her spy mages set up at various precise sections of the banquet hall which was supposed to accommodate individuals attending the ceremony both locally and internationally and explosives attached to this location, she was all set but before that Dorcana was too be saved.

With support from inside, she was able to gain access into the college grounds, took out the guards guarding the Serac post and cloak spell some of her members to appear as one so as not to create room for suspicion. Casting a teleportation spell, out she came with her remaining cult members on to the fields of Serac. It was a familiar ground because she once guarded this place and imprisoned some of the monsters that were locked up there. Down they went into the cave like structure and past the void like door.

"To whom do I owe this pleasure" Dorcana said in a still voice.
"Nobody but your humble servants my lord, your way still lives and we your children are here to take back the saviour of the mage society" Wendy replied.
"Execute this child and you'll taste power like you have never seen before" Dorcana said with an evil smile on his face.

Now getting someone out from a black crystal was no child's play as it required immense power of which Wendy hadn't ascertained yet and even if she had, would still require support from mages alike. But she was aware

of this and so she had to do this manually making use of a sabre tooth jack saw and in executing this she needed time which seemed not to be favouring her cause unfortunately extra security spells were put in check mostly at the Serac post and this had worn off the cloaking spell she had created which made her members discoverable to the mage special forces who were on patrol at that point, and after much torturing they were able to get the truth and were headed for her direction. She could feel their presence getting closer and closer, she was almost done, and all she needed was just little time.
We'll buy you enough time said her available cult members as they noticed the situation and that they did but at the expenses of their lives. Wendy was able to teleport successfully to the mountain tops with Dorcana but at present she had a heavy heart for the lives she had lost.

"Their sacrifices will not be in vain" Dorcana assured her "we must leave now my child" he added.
But she wasn't going to leave without setting off those explosives and out from her pocket she brought forth the detonator and with tears in her eyes, click it went.

Now Michael and the gang fortunately had decided to turn up late for the ceremony but Michael could feel something off and fuzzy, it was more like an urge for him to leave and attend the ceremony.

" emmmm guys am sorry, I can't wait I'll see you all at the ceremony" he said as he ran out towards the banquet hall, his heart was heavy, he could feel something bad about to happen and just as stepped into the banquet down to the middle floor he was quick to notice the explosive attached to the pillars.

"everybody gets down" he shouted as he created an immense dome of air which ripped a lot of energy from him.

(Boom) went the whole building as fire swarm throughout the whole dome but Michael was determined to hold the dome and with support from fellow air mages they were able to hold off the flames till it subsided and down he went. All he could hear were whispers and whispers until he heard people shouting "he is an outcast, he has exhibited more than one elemental powers according to our students testimonies, seize him!!!!" and unconscious he went immediately.

To be continued.

ABOUT THE AUTHOR

Samson Excel is an undergraduate student from the University of Nsukka, Nigeria and also an indigene of Nigeria. He wishes to share his knowledge on certain issues concerning communication and understanding among spouse.

For more information on when the release of The Journey of the Mage Outcast Book 2 will be released, you can follow me on my social media platforms for updates.

@Divxce on twitter

@Divxcel on Instagram

www.ingramcontent.com/pod-product-compliance
Lightning Source LLC
Chambersburg PA
CBHW071121240526
45465CB00022B/752